187209

PowerKids Readers:

The Bilingual Library of the United States of America™

ARIZONA

VANESSA BROWN

TRADUCCIÓN AL ESPAÑOL: MARÍA CRISTINA BRUSCA

The Rosen Publishing Group's
PowerKids Press™ & **Editorial Buenas Letras**™
New York

Published in 2005 by The Rosen Publishing Group, Inc.
29 East 21st Street, New York, NY 10010

First Edition

Photo Credits: Cover © Craig Aurness/Corbis; p.5 © Joseph Sohm; Visions of America/Corbis; pp.5 (inset), 30 © One Mile Up, Inc.;pp.9, 31 (desert) © Scott T. Smith/Corbis; pp.11, 30, 31 (Grand Canyon) © Craig Aurness/Corbis; p.13 ©B.S.P.I./Corbis; pp.15,31 (Chavez) © Bettmann/Corbis; p.17 Arizona State Library, Archives and Public Records, Archives Division, Phoenix, #97-7014; p.19 © Charles Mauzy/Corbis; p.21 © Phil Schermeister/Corbis; pp.23, 31 (observatory) © Roger Ressmeyer/Corbis; pp.25, 30 (Phoenix)© Richard Cummins/Corbis; p.30 (turquoise) © Richard T.Nowitz/Corbis; p.30 (cactus blossom) © Index Stock, Inc.; p.30 (cactus wren) © Darrell Gulin/Corbis; p.30 (Palo Verde) © Eric and David Hosking/Corbis;p.31(Geronimo) © Corbis; p.31(McCain) © Reuters/Corbis; p.31(O'Connor) © Wally McNamee/Corbis; p.31(Cooper) © Lynn Goldsmith/Corbis; p. 31 (court) © Joseph Sohm; ChromoSohm Inc./Corbis

Library of Congress Cataloging-in-Publication Data

Brown, Vanessa, 1963–
Arizona / Vanessa Brown.– 1st ed.
p. cm. – (The bilingual library of the United States of America) Includes index.
ISBN 1-4042-3067-X (library binding)
1. Arizona–Juvenile literature. I. Title. II. Series.
F811.3.B76 2005
979.1–dc22

2004028759

Manufactured in the United States of America

Due to the changing nature of Internet links, Editorial Buenas Letras has developed an online list of Web sites related to the subject of this book. This site is updated regularly. Please use this link to access the list:

http://www.buenasletraslinks.com/ls/arizona

Contents

Contenido

Welcome to Arizona

Arizona is the sixth-largest state in the United States. Arizona is known as the Grand Canyon State.

Bienvenidos a Arizona

Por su tamaño, Arizona es el sexto estado de los Estados Unidos. Arizona se conoce como el Estado del Gran Cañón.

The Arizona Flag and the State Seal

La bandera y el escudo de Arizona

Arizona Geography

Arizona borders the states of California, Nevada, Utah, Colorado, and New Mexico. Arizona also shares a border with the country of Mexico.

Geografía de Arizona

Arizona limita con los estados de California, Nevada, Utah, Colorado y Nuevo México. Arizona también comparte una frontera con otro país: México.

Arizona is called the land of sunshine. Most of Arizona's land is made up of deserts. These organ pipe cacti are in the Sonoran Desert.

Arizona se conoce como la tierra donde brilla el sol. La mayor parte del territorio de Arizona son desiertos. Éstos cactos "tubo de órgano" están en el Desierto de Sonora.

A View of the Organ Pipe National Monument

Vista del Monumento Nacional Organ Pipe

Arizona is home to the Grand Canyon. A canyon is a deep valley with steep sides. The Colorado River runs through the bottom of the Grand Canyon.

En Arizona se encuentra el Gran Cañón. Un cañón es un valle profundo con paredes muy altas. Por el fondo del Gran Cañón corre el Río colorado.

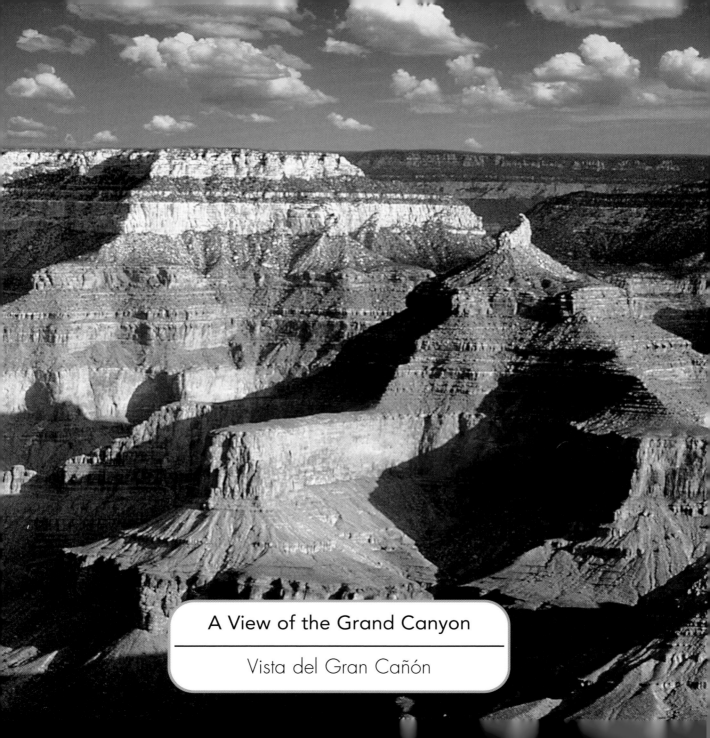

A View of the Grand Canyon

Vista del Gran Cañón

Arizona History

Arizonians are proud of their rich Native American history. The state has many Native American groups, like the Hopi and the Navajo.

Historia de Arizona

Los arizonianos están muy orgullosos de su rica historia nativoamericana. El estado es el hogar de muchos grupos de nativos americanos como los hopi y los navajo.

Navajo Indians in Arizona

Indios navajo en Arizona

Cochise was an Apache chief. He fought to guard the land in Arizona where his people lived. The Apache were strong fighters.

Cochise fue un jefe apache. Cochise luchó para defender la tierra de Arizona donde vivía su pueblo. Los apaches fueron guerreros valientes.

Cochise

Lorna Lockwood worked at the Arizona Supreme Court in the 1960s. She was the first woman in the United States to lead a state supreme court.

Lorna Lockwood trabajó en la Suprema Corte de Arizona en los años ´60. Lockwood fue la primera mujer presidente de una corte suprema, de un estado de los Estados Unidos.

Lorna Lockwood

Living in Arizona

Arizona is home to many Hispanics. Hispanics are people from Spanish-speaking countries. Many Hispanic fiestas include dance and music.

La vida en Arizona

Arizona es hogar de muchos hispanos. Los hispanos son personas que vienen de países donde se habla español. Muchas fiestas hispanas se celebran con danza y música.

Hispanic Boys and Girls Dressed for a Fiesta

Niños y niñas hispanos con sus trajes de fiesta

Most of Arizona's fun takes place outdoors. Hiking, golfing, and snow skiing are popular activities. In the Salt River, people enjoy many water sports.

La mayoría de las diversiones en Arizona tienen lugar al aire libre. Las caminatas, el golf y esquiar en nieve son actividades muy populares. En el río Salt, la gente disfruta de los deportes acuáticos.

Arizonians Enjoy the Salt River, Outside Phoenix.

Los arizonianos disfrutan del río Salt, cerca de Phoenix.

Arizona Today

The clear weather in Arizona is good for observing the night sky. There are many observatories around the city of Tucson. This area is called the Astronomy Capital of the World.

Arizona, hoy

El clima en Arizona es bueno para explorar el espacio por la noche. Hay muchos observatorios alrededor de la ciudad de Tucson. Esta área es conocida como la capital mundial de la astronomía.

Kitt Peak National Observatory

Observatorio nacional Kitt Peak

Tucson, Chandler, Mesa, Glendale and Tempe are important cities in Arizona. Phoenix is Arizona's largest city. It is also the capital of the state.

Tucson, Chandler, Mesa, Glendale y Tempe son ciudades importantes de Arizona. Phoenix es la ciudad más grande de Arizona y también es la capital del estado.

The Capitol Building in Phoenix

Capitolio en la cuidad de Phoenix

Activity:
Let's Draw Arizona's Flag

Actividad:
Dibujemos la bandera de Arizona

1

Draw a rectangle.

Dibuja un rectángulo.

2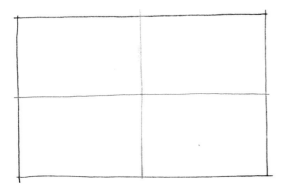

Draw one vertical line and one horizontal line inside the rectangle.

Dibuja una línea vertical y una línea horizontal adentro del rectángulo.

3

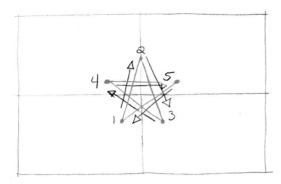

Draw a five-pointed star in the middle of your flag.

Dibuja una estrella de cinco puntas en el medio de tu bandera.

4

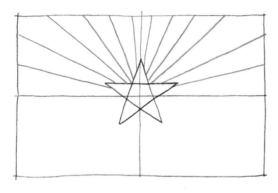

Great job! Now draw 12 lines from the star to the edges of the flag.

¡Muy bien! Ahora dibuja 12 líneas desde la estrella hasta los bordes de la bandera.

5

Erase the lines in the star and the vertical line. Color the flag.

Borra la línea vertical y las líneas de adentro de la estrella. Colorea tu bandera.

Timeline		Cronología
Native Americans arrive in what is now Arizona	**12,000 BC /AC**	Los nativos americanos llegan a lo que hoy es Arizona.
Marcos de Niza is the first white person to enter the region.	**1539**	Marcos de Niza es el primer hombre blanco en llegar a la región.
Arizona becomes part of Mexico.	**1821**	Arizona pasa a formar parte de México.
The United States and Mexico go to war.	**1846**	Comienza la guerra entre los Estados Unidos y México.
John Wesley Powell explores the Grand Canyon.	**1869**	John Wesley Powell explora el Gran Cañón.
Arizona becomes a state.	**1912**	Arizona se convierte en un estado.
Arizona Native Americans win the right to vote.	**1948**	Los nativos americanos de Arizona ganan su derecho a votar.
Raúl Castro becomes the first Mexican American governor of Arizona.	**1975**	Raúl Castro se convierte en el primer gobernador mexicoamericano de Arizona.

Arizona Events	Eventos en Arizona
January Arizona National Livestock Show in Phoenix	Enero Exposición Arizona National Livestock, en Phoenix
February La Fiesta de los Vaqueros Rodeo in Tucson	Febrero Rodeo *La fiesta de los Vaqueros*, en Tucson
May Wyatt Earp Days in Tombstone Cinco de Mayo celebrations (May 5th)	Mayo Día de Wyatt Earp, en Tombstone Celebraciones del Cinco de Mayo (5 de mayo)
June Country Music Festival in Payson Arizona's Garlic Festival in Sedona	Junio Festival de música country, en Payson Festival del ajo de Arizona, en Sedona
July Frontier Days in Prescott	Julio Días de la frontera, en Prescott
September Navajo Tribal Fair in Window Rock	Septiembre Feria de la tribu navajo, en Window Rock
November Annual Hot Air Balloon Races in Glendale	Noviembre Competencia anual de globos, en Glendale
December-January Fiesta Bowl Sport Festival	Diciembre-Enero Festival Fiesta Bowl Sport

29

Arizona Facts/Datos sobre Arizona

<u>Population</u>
5 million

<u>Población</u>
5 millones

<u>Capital</u>
Phoenix

<u>Capital</u>
Phoenix

<u>State Motto</u>
God Enriches

<u>Lema del estado</u>
Dios enriquece

<u>State Flower</u>
Saguaro Cactus Blossom

<u>Flor del estado</u>
Flor del cacto Saguaro

<u>State Bird</u>
Cactus Wren

<u>Ave del estado</u>
Reyezuelo del cacto

<u>State Nickname</u>
Grand Canyon State

<u>Mote del estado</u>
Estado del Gran Cañón

<u>State Tree</u>
Palo Verde

<u>Árbol del estado</u>
Palo verde

<u>State Song</u>
"Arizona"

<u>Canción del estado</u>
"Arizona"

<u>State Gemstone</u>
Turquoise

<u>Piedra preciosa</u>
Turquesa

Famous Arizonians/Arizonianos famosos

Cochise
(1800?–1874)

Apache Chief
Jefe apache

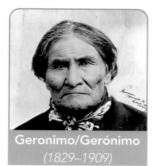

Geronimo/Gerónimo
(1829–1909)

Apache Chief
Jefe apache

César Chávez
(1927–1993)

Labor leader
Líder de los trabajadores

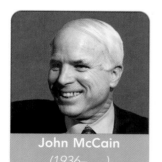

John McCain
(1936–   )

U.S. Senator
Senador de E.U.A.

Sandra Day O' Connor
(1930–   )

Supreme Court Justice
Juez de la Suprema Corte

Alice Cooper
(1964–   )

Singer
Cantante

Words to Know/Palabras que debes saber

canyon
cañón

court
corte

desert
desierto

observatory
observatorio

Here are more books to read about Arizona:
Otros libros que puedes leer sobre Arizona:

In English/En inglés:
Arizona
Rookie Read-About Geography
by: Aki Becker, Michelle
Children's Press, 2004

In Spanish/En español:
Arizona
Rookie Español
by: Aki Becker, Michelle
Children's Press, 2004

Words in English: 257

Palabras en español: 299

Index

Índice